BEAT GENER ATION

BEAT GENERATION

3-Act Play

Jack Kerouac

Jack Kerouac
c/o Sterling Lord
15 East 48th St
New York 17, NY
PLaza 1-2533

INTRODUCTION BY A. M. HOMES

THUNDER'S MOUTH PRESS
NEW YORK

BEAT GENERATION

Published by
Thunder's Mouth Press
An Imprint of Avalon Publishing Group Inc.
245 West 17th Street, 11th Floor
New York, NY 10011

First printing October 2005

Library of Congress Cataloging-in-Publication Data is available.

ISBN 1-56025-742-3
ISBN 13: 978-1-56025-742-4

9 8 7 6 5 4 3 2 1

Book design by Maria Elias
Printed in the United States
Distributed by Publishers Group West

Introduction

In order to talk about it you have to put it into some sort of a cultural context—it was 1957, Dwight D. Eisenhower was president, Richard M. Nixon vice president, the Pulitzer Prize in drama went to Eugene O'Neill's *Long Day's Journey into Night,* no fiction award was given. *West Side Story* opened on Broadway, *Leave It to Beaver* premiered on television, and if you were going to the movies chances are it was to see *The Bridge on the River Kwai, Twelve Angry Men,* or *Peyton Place.* On the home front there was still a struggle to integrate the schools, while the Russians launched *Sputnik I* and the Space Age began. It was 1957, and Jack Kerouac's *On the Road* was published—other books that year included Bernard Malamud's *The Assistant,* James Agee's *A Death in the Family,* and Noam Chomsky's *Syntactic Structures.*

At this point, Kerouac and his band of scribes were all about embracing and celebrating this "beat" life. Kerouac himself had already coined the term, according to some accounts as early as 1948, suggesting societal conventions were "beat," "tired," "worn-out." Many have suggested that Kerouac's use of the term "Beat Generation" evolved from being a postwar reference to Hemingway's "Lost Generation" to a more positive label: the Beats were enlightened, "beatific" ones—a nice confluence of the Buddhist and Catholic philosophies that were so important to Kerouac.

In 1957, Kerouac wasn't yet what he is today—a figure as or more dominant in contemporary culture as the faces on Mount Rushmore. In 1957, he still had the benefit of a certain anonymity—he was still, for the moment, the purest version of Jack Kerouac, not a personality, not a celebrity.

Unlike the World War II vets who came home, got married, moved to suburbia, and fully embraced the American Dream and the blossoming culture of more, more, more, keeping up with the Joneses and then some, the Beat life was lived on the edges. Beats had nothing to lose and not far to fall. Holy men, meditators, anti-materialists, they were the exact opposite of "Company Men." Kerouac and his experimental fraternity aspired to something else—a kind of freedom. They wanted to soar, to fly, to move through time and space unfettered. They wanted to find spirituality and deliverance among the dispossessed. And they wanted to have a good time, win a few bucks on the horses, have some drinks, and get laid. Compared to the average Joe they were wild—awe-inspiring and threatening.

Kerouac's style was not just philosophically bold; it was linguistic guerilla warfare—a literary atom bomb smashing everything. On one side of him were the hyperintellectual Beckett and Joyce. On the other, the antiacademic: Hemingway, Anderson, and Dos Passos. Kerouac absorbed it all and went beyond.

In order to make sense of this play you have to keep it in perspective. It's now 2005, a line of Jack Kerouac clothing is about to be released, the manuscript of *On the Road* is on tour across America. A few months ago, in a New Jersey warehouse this "new" play by Kerouac was discovered—three acts, written in 1957, and typed up by Kerouac's ever-loving mother, Gabrielle, also known as "Mémère."

The play was never produced—at the time there was a lot of interest but no action. In a letter Kerouac wrote he described his interest in theater and film in this way:

> What I wanta do is re-do the theater and the cinema in America, give it a spontaneous dash, remove pre-conceptions of "situation" and let people rave on as they do in real life. That's what

> the play is: no plot in particular, no "meaning" in particular, just the way people are. Everything I write I do in the spirit where I imagine myself an Angel returned to earth seeing it with sad eyes as it is.

The play *Beat Generation* marks a wonderful addition to the Kerouac oeuvre. It will be great fun to see what happens with it—I can easily imagine it being performed and each staging being incredibly different from the last—it's all about what you bring to it.

It is a play of its time—which is why context is important. In bits and pieces it is reminiscent of Tennessee Williams, Clifford Odets, and a bit of Arthur Miller. But by comparison to those playwrights whose work is formal and well defined, this play is loose, unfettered, it is about juxtaposition, relation, words and ideas bouncing off one another, riffing in a bebop scatter.

Beat Generation opens in the early morning in an apartment near the Bowery, with drinking—the reverie of the first glass. It is a man's world—these working men, brakemen for the railroad, drinking men, who spend their day off betting on horses, men who swear by saying "durnit," men who have a girl waiting on them, warming their coffee—women's liberation never made it into Kerouac's world. It is set in a disappeared New York City, with the smoky scent of cigarettes hanging over all, men playing chess, the racket of the elevated subways, the feel of life lived underground, everything a little bit beat. And *Beat Generation* is pervaded by the music of conversation.

Working in spurts, Kerouac spewed this "spontaneous bop prosody," or "jazz poetry." The play (and the novels) are everything and the kitchen sink too. It is a kind of demolition derby pileup, a jazzy musical of words picking up speed and hurling themselves forward—in a bumper car version of dialogue. *Beat Generation* is about talking and friendship and shooting the shit, it is about the biggest question of all—existence. Kerouac and his rough-hewn characters—just this side of hobos—want to know how and why we exist and then in some spontaneous combustion they come to know that in the end there are no answers, there is just the moment we are in, and the people around us.

Here is the romance of the road, rebirth and karma—Kerouac's peculiar and deeply personal combination of the working man discussing astral bodies, karmic debt, past lives, and the selling of Jesus. Here is the power of ideas and the difficulty of escaping belief. And here is the love of god and the fear of god—despite Kerouac's interest in the alternative, his exploration of Buddhism and Eastern philosophies, he could never escape his Catholic upbringing.

Yet the play has a masculine swagger, a brand of bravado. Language and characters careen off each other, in a kind of doped deliciousness, in which one feels the heat of an afternoon, the smell of hay and shit and beer at the racetrack, the greasy squeal of brakes, and the kind of down-and-dirty that never really washes off.

Kerouac was the man who allowed writers to enter the world of flow—different from stream-of-consciousness, his philosophy was about being in the current, open to possibility, allowing creativity to move through you, and you to be one with both process and content. It was about embracing experience rather than resisting; it is in fact the very roman candle Kerouac writes about in *On the Road.*

On a more personal note—without Kerouac, without Jimi Hendrix, without Mark Rothko, there would be no me. I used to think Jack Kerouac was my father (sometimes literally) and Susan Sontag was my mother. I could diagram out one hell of a family tree, with Henry Miller and Eugene O'Neill as my uncles and so on. Kerouac raised me spiritually, psychologically, creatively—he gave me permission to exist.

In the end, *Beat Generation* is a treat, a sweet found under a sofa cushion. For those of us who never had enough Kerouac, now there is more.

—A. M. Homes
New York, June 2005

A note to the reader:
The printed version of Beat Generation *conforms as exactly as posssible to the original typescript, complete with Kerouac's own inimitable punctuation, spelling, and made-up words.*

ACT ONE

(SCENE IS EARLY MORNING IN NEW YORK NEAR THE BOWERY, STANDING IN THE KITCHEN, CHEAP KITCHEN, ARE A COLORED GUY CALLED JULE AND A WHITE GUY CALLED BUCK, AND THEY'RE BOTH RAISING GLASSES OF WINE TO EACH OTHER. IN LITTLE GLASSES, AND BUCK'S SAYING:)

BUCK

Alright Jule, let's have one

JULE

I wonder what the vintner buys, one half so precious as what he sells . . .

BUCK

Wow! . . . give us another one . . . Hey you drink fast!

JULE

Drink! for tomorrow you may be one with yesterday's 7,000 years . . .

BUCK

But that's not right, you didn't get the whole thing there. ain't you got any others?

JULE

Not now . . . sit, man

BUCK

Alright Jule . . . Here I am sitting in Jullius Chauncey's kitchen in a clear cool morning in October 1955, the freshness of the day's first jug, ugh. . You know Jule, there's nothing, there's no way to recreate the effect of that first glass which you get in the morning when you wake up, yet, all over the world drinkers will gobble gobble and bulp . . . they want more more more of what they can't have, because it can only happen once . . . isnt that right? . .Let's have another quote, Jule

JULE

No I'm tired

BUCK

Well here we go, let's have another one (DRINKING) . . . I wonder where Milo is

(THE DOOR OPENS AND IN WALKS MILO, WHO IS A MEDIUM HEIGHT DARK HAIRED FELLOW IN A FULL BRAKEMAN'S UNIFORM, HAT, CAP, THE BLUE UNIFORM THE RACING FORM IN ONE POCKET, THE BIBLE AND OTHER BOOKS IN ANOTHER POCKET, AND A FEW FLUTES STICKING OUT OF HIS POCKET, FOLLOWED BY ANOTHER BRAKEMAN BUT HE'S SIX*FOOT*SIX FULLY CLEANLY DRESSED AND SHAVED, IN FULL CONDUCTOR UNIFORM, FOLLOWED BY A LITTLE TINY FOUR-FOOT-ELEVEN NOT QUITE MIDGET IN A FULL SUIT WITH VEST, HATLESS . . . THEY ARE MILO, SLIM, AND TOMMY)

BUCK

Hey there you are, I knew you'd get here . . . Well well well look at all these brakemen's uniforms here . . . Winos and brakemen getting together early in the morning, hey?

TOMMY

Hey there Buck, what you say boy? . . . Say can I sit at the table Vicki?

(—AS A GIRL, WHITE GIRL, COMES IN FROM THE OTHER ROOM, HAVING HEARD THE VISITORS ARRIVE—)

Can I sit at the table and dope out these horses? Today I've got a couple horses running at Jamaica I'd give my left arm if I could go out and play them at the track but there's a little matter of a job at Riker's at 2 o'clock durnit

MILO

Alright Tommy . . . you move over the end there Tommy m'boy, that's right Buck sits on the floor so's me and old long tall Slim Summerville here can resume our best four-out-of-seven series championship chips chess game of the world (LOOKING AT VICKI) . . Ah just what I like to see in the morning, boys and girls. You got any coffee Vicki?

VICKI

Yes I have some, I'll warm it up here

MILO

Just a little bit of sugar in that coffee Vicki m'dear

VICKI

Yes *sir*

MILO

Well now listen here, old buddy Buck, (TAKING OUT THE CHESSBOARD AND PIECES), so it's true as you do say, that God *is* us, is just us, right here, now, exactly as you say, we don't have to run to God because we're already there, yet Buck really now face it old buddy that sonumbitch trail to Heaven is a *long* trail . . .

BUCK

Wal, that's just words . . .

MILO

Boy we start out in our astral bodies, man, and you know the way a ghost go when headin out there to that bright blank night go in a straight line, that, and then, as he wanders, just astral-born and new to the game he gets to wigglin and a-goin from side to side, that is, to explore, much as H. G. Wells says about a maid sweepin out a hall from side to side, the way migrations advance? . . .

VICKI

What are you *talkin* about again!

MILO

And so Astral, he'll go migrate out there to the next or Martian level where he bumps into all them *levels* you see, but with that spectral astral special interprenation . . . how do you pronounce that, inter-pe-ne-tration speed

BUCK

Words

MILO

True . . . true . . . but then after—now lay out these things Slim, I'll take the—I'll tell you what we'll do, I'll take the black, you take the white, I'm going to give you a chance today so now listen Buck, here was a guy who had such a bad aura of traitorship around him, in fact he was a later entity of Judas, he'd, or people'd sense him, sense him and turn in the street and say "Who's that *betrayer* just went by?" all of his life suffering from some curse people had of him, which was that karmic debt he had to pay for selling Jesus for a handful of silver . . .

BUCK

Words . . . I keep saying "words" Milo and I really mean it, I'm trying to get you to say "God is Words" . . . It's *still* all words, ain't it?

MILO

No no no no no no no no no no no . . . When that astral body gets to Saturn certain conditions there may seek . . might get to change him into a rock and so on, you gotta watch out boy, you want him to turn into a rock?

BUCK

Tell me seriously Milo, doesnt the entity go to God in Heaven?

MILO

That it does, after a long trail and trial, you see . . . hmm (LIGHTING A CIGARETTE SUAVELY)

BUCK

Ah words

MILO

Words as you will

BUCK

Or birds . . .

MILO

Till finally, purified and so spotless to be like the garment that was never rented, the entity *does* arrive in Heaven and back to God, so is why I say we're not there now.

BUCK

How can we help not being there now? We cant be anywhere else . . . the world, or Heaven, is what form is . . . We cant avoid our reward . . . Heaven so sure, Milo

MILO

Ahh . . . . Alright Slim your move, you're white

TOMMY

Hey Milo you wanta look at the sheets I worked out?

MILO

No, I dont have to look at anything, I tell you I've got it made

JULE

The horses? . . . You've got the horses made, how you got it made?

MILO

Sit down here Slim, and we'll take out these, ah . . . we'll take out a fielding lance at each other's hide . . . Pawn to king four? by God I know how to answer you, I'll lay my bible here beside me in case I got something to quote to old Buck there sittin on the floor that unbeliever . . . Vicki you got that coffee ready yet, just a little bit of sugar, you know, nothin fancy, unless Buck wants to run out and buy pork chops with that w-i-n-e money he's about to run out with and buy wine

BUCK

No no no, you look over all the form charts for the day, find only horses that have won 33 percent of their races, and especially run within the last eight days dropping weight *and* running their favorite distance, several other items . . . .

MILO

Pawn to king four, hey? . . . .Well we'll try knight here, we'll try knight here

SLIM

Knight to bishop five

BUCK

How many times Milo have I told you you cant beat the horses, my father lost his *business* doin it man . . . . 'course years later he kept sayin that he lost his business on account of some flood or other but . . . it was that old mutuel flood, boy

MILO

Yass yass yass, your move big buddy

TOMMY

Running a mile and a sixteenth in 1:43 flat comes to a mile and an eighth today, I dont know, I dont know if he can stand another . . . another half a furlong

BUCK

Bearing impost of seventeen hundred thousand million pounds he will find sumpin . . . .

MILO

Lazy Charley, Lazy Charley, why you, man, dont you realize they found that guy dead on the racetrack with forty thousand dollars worth of uncashed tickets in his pocket, he had em so figured out—now wait a minute now man, now look here—honey that's right, just a little bit of sugar, that's right, fine

VICKI

Eggs?

MILO

Eggs, eggs . . . . fine, fine, fine, FINE . . . . hmm, it's better than Chinatown

VICKI

Anybody else?

MILO

Sunnyside up and a bit of hot strong coffee to go with it, you know, make some more coffee and I like it pipin hot

JULE

(SINGING BOP) Swap swapa diddleya deel do

TOMMY

There oughta be a hole in there for him to sneak through, you know?

JULE

Did you find my pussy last night Tommy, huh Tommy did you find a nice little old broad lyin on the sidewalk and take her to you know, you know, your pad

TOMMY

Not last night Jule, I was—I just had a few beers in the Pink Angel and there was a couple of old gals there but they didnt appeal to me too much, too drunk

JULE

Did you make it with any big old broads last night Tommy? did you did you did you did you *did* you?

VICKI

Oh Jule!

JULE

Swing, somebody, swing!

BUCK

Yeah

JULE

Yeah

MILO

Well now old Lazy Charley see—

SLIM

—alright I'll move this bishop—

MILO

—he gets up there in the club lounge you know, and he's comin post time, he's standin there by the fifty dollar window and the warning buzzer rings, Old Charley takes one casual look to see who's third choice and lays the money *down* . . . . That's why I wanta go to the racetrack today because man I tell *you*,—and dont you see really it's all really worked out for us in advance and all we gotta do is pile right on . . . . that's why I say I wanta go to that racetrack today, I gotta win that money back, and besides—the money I lost, you know—and there's something I want you to know, how many times have I gone to that bettin window and asked the man for number five because somebody just then said "number five" and the ticket I'd originally wanted was number two, and I'm standin there you know and I'm lookin around, and instead of buyin my number two which goes accordin to Lazy Charley's system I buy number five

BUCK

Why dont you just say "Give me number two instead of number five, I made a mistake" . . . . wouldn't he give it back to you? the guy that sells the tickets there?

MILO

Hmm, well . . . . because there was a disincarnate entity telling me number five, I believe that it was trying to help—

BUCK

Sometimes you just hear them in your head?

MILO

Yeh, and it may be trying to let me win or lose with the certainty of the foreknowledge of the outcome of that race, old buddy, dont you think I dont know, why pshaw boy, I got—and you know Lazy Charley never said he was ever gonna deviate from that third choice

BUCK

So at least you know that disembodied ghost entities are trying to make you lost because you say that the third choice cant fail!

MILO

Cant

VICKI

What do they look like?

BUCK

What?

VICKI

The dis-arnate eninnies . . . . the disarnate entities there

MILO

All kinds of ways . . . . auras, auras, say for instance that betrayer that I told you about there, scared everybody down down the street, auras that are showin ogres of the imagination opers anyway and he's runnin down the street there, everybody knew that in a previous lifetime he had been a great betrayer, and he carried that along with him as he went along—

BUCK

Yeah, big seedy ghosts amplin down the line into that endless sky, shoot, man, Milo why, what are you talkin about

MILO

Now look you just listen to me boy and I'm gonna show you somethin, hm, boy and you know that Jesus Christ he comes down and his karma on earth is to know that he is the son of God assigned to die for the safety, the eternal safety of mankind, it's all arranged ahead of time, even Judas . .

BUCK

Well, and all the lives of *ants* are arranged ahead of time?

MILO

No, not ants. Knowing it, Jesus, he does it, dies on the

cross, that was his karma as Jesus, dont you understand? . . . dig what that means . . .

BUCK

Okay

MILO

So, ah, back to Lazy Charley . . . . you see now that cool Charley he didnt have to sweat and jump in the crowd, men . . . . . . he collects his uncashed tickets—

BUCK

—and dies

MILO

Yeah that's right, and from there he goes on to whatever his karma demands of him . . . er, the next planet, or the next aura, wherever he has to go next he'll do it . . . Aint nothin worrying him . . . Came on earth to devise a system to beat the horses and left earth.

BUCK

What's this book here you got?

MILO

That's Edgar Cayce . . .

BUCK

That's Edgar Cayce, you know about Edgar Cayce, Jule, old Okie guy you know come in a house with someone sick, and goes by the bed of the sick person and loosens his tie and gets down on the couch flat on his back, and there's his wife sittin by the bed with a pad and pencil and there's this sick person there, see, and old Cayce goes into a trance, finally she says "Edgar!" as he goes into his trance, "why does Midget Bloobloo got thrombophlebitis in this hardass earth, what's he done to deserve it and how is he going to cure it?"

MILO

That's right

SLIM

What's this?

BUCK

Edgar Cayce . . . see, and Edgar Cayce lyin there and says: "Edgar Dwapdwap here in a previous lifetime—"

MILO

Previous lifetime that's right . . . . white moves

BUCK

"—was a Aztec priest in the hills of old Teotihuacan where

they shed his pumpin heart, he shed more blood of victims and drank it by the buckets and blood and sawdust and saw fires, finally now to atone for those sins he's been reborn with an excess of blood that thickens the clots in his veins and makes it work his karma, his earned fate, his fate he earned, by suffering now, he has to pay back for that, and that's why he has this blood disease . . ." So that, and then—

TOMMY

Hey, there's a bloodclot in this egg!

MILO

Throw it away!

TOMMY

That's a little chicken in there, I aint gonna throw it away . . .

BUCK

How come that this Edgar Cayce never predicted the horses?

MILO

Because, man, that is another, and that is a different kind of information now, now he cured the guy with sickness, like you say, he discovered why he had it, and then he gave him the cure, which was whatever it was, because this information otherwise that—he *could*—have predicted the horses but didnt, or wouldnt, because it was forbidden information, you'll hear all about that tonight old buddy when you and I my day's totals are at least run off, the whole thing mathematically should be ready tomorrow, *one*, we tie up that train boy and get in my car where Irwin, you and Paul be waitin, and I suppose this Manuel's comin to the track with us, aint he, and Paul—and so we'll drive out to my pad out there, and the Bishop's comin tonight to give us all a polite talk

TOMMY

The bishop? Bishop Who?

MILO

The Bishop Hartori there . . .

SLIM

Ah you mean the guy Cora goes to hear

MILO

Yeah, you know, that—give him my—My God she gave him my only good floor lamp, cant even see in the livingroom anymore, hmm

BUCK

Floor lamp? For what?

MILO

Well, for his lecture hall

BUCK

What church is this guy?

MILO

Oh it's the ref—the new, ah, Aramaean church I believe they call it

BUCK

And you mean we're all going to have to see this guy tonight?

MILO

In my house

BUCK

What is he wearing?

MILO

Well, he wears long black robes, and he has a big crucifix hanging down . . . . just a young kid 28, real hepcat . . . . He's gonna be there with his old aunts, you know . . .

BUCK

And Irwin . . . . Paul . . . and all these people?

MILO

Yeah, and you, and . . . others. Oh, Cora moppin up the house and gettin ready all day and sendin out postcards and being all excited and lookin for more lamps . . .

BUCK

Well, ah, by God, I aint—I'm lookin forward to the race-track but what am I gonna do with a *Bishop*

MILO

Oh show him anything you want, and explain to him the fact—in fact he knows all about that, man, why shit that guy there aint nothin he dont know about . . . . Aurobindo, y'know

VICKI

Jule, I havent got enough plates

MILO

That's alright baby put it all in one plate and we'll split right down the middle and sideways and as many's people gonna eat and just chew off

BUCK

And me drunk, already drunk last night with Maguire and only just had a few hours on Jule's couch and to meet the

Bishop? Do I have to be on my best behavior? what am I gonna do and the racetrack too?

TOMMY

Ah what are you complainin about Buck, you have a pretty nice life, I never seen you sweat for much

BUCK

I sweat for what I sweat for. Listen Milo, where's Irwin now?

MILO

He'll meet us at the car at six-fifteen when we take the race-track train back, we tie it up, and I'm off duty

TOMMY

Chesterfield will win the sixth race, by God I'm gonna place a bet on him

MILO

That third choice hasnt—bishop to rook five—that third choice for two days stopped and that is exactly seventeen races he missed now, now he's bound *deadbang* sure to come in today no doubt about it and if he misses it'll be 25 straight and I aint never heard of that yet at Jamaica, or anywhere, though Lazy Charley did say in that article that they had there in Turf or somethin, he'll sometimes miss as much as thirty straight and boy that's when you gotta have that *reserve* in the bank, and faith

JULE

Ah, why do you wanta make a while lot of money anyway, I mean everybody likes money but that's all you *talk* about, man . . . . Here you are working on the railroad making 650 dollars a month and you have your chick, and your pad, and your kids, and you just keep talking and talkin about *money*

MILO

It isnt for *money*, no sir, not at all, it's philanthropy. Now Buck here you cover the California tracks, see, I'll—I'll wire him the money and—the New England tracks that is—and Tommy the Florida tracks, see Ole Tommy out there runnin around pattin the asses of all them young girls down there in Florida? We'll get old Jule here to cover the Chicago tracks near St. Louis so he can be close to home there and see all his old broads there . . . . and down in New Orleans we'll send out Irwin there, soon as I learn him to do this properly and play the system, gotta wait you know till the last minute with his eyeballs glued to that toteboard and, old rubber number two's gonna have to send him, Paul there? his buddy, we're gonna have to send him to Russia to cover them Russian tracks out there, and get some Mexican cat to cover Aguascalientes boy, and pretty soon we'll send Marlon Brando to cover tracks in France or somethin, have a network of buddies, million dollar organization, we can build up soup kitchens, monasteries, devote all that karma you see, work out our karma and go off when we die with somethin that will enable us to go off into the future, our future life in outer space, with some new kind of—*credit*—and turn all that around, 'cause you know man there's not enough time for all the things that's got to be done, not enough *money*, only do you realize—sonumbitch that pawn has got to go! (PFUIT, SWEEPING OFF PAWN)—Say kid do you need any help with those eggs there baby? um, hah? what's the idea of giving the eggs to Tommy first, just because he's smaller than I am dont mean that I'm not as hungry as he is, you know

JULE

Buck go out and get that next poorboy

BUCK

I still need three more cents. Milo give me a nickle

MILO

I'll give you a nickle and tomorrow providing I'm sending you to Jamaica to contrive that line, boy, that third choice dont hit today it's *bound* to hit tomorrow you see, we go out today together . . . . if it misses today you've got to be out there *dead sure* tomorrow and get on that percentage!

BUCK

Okay Milo, that's sure

MILO

Now I'm gonna give you three hundred dollars tomorrow, and 38 cents for a poorboy pint of wine that you can drink on a hay stack when the races are done

BUCK

Yeah I'll be drinkin on a haystack when the races are done, watchin jockeys drivin away in Cadillacs, and airplanes landing at Idlewild

MILO

That's right boy, and airplanes landing at Idlewild with all that money in the sky

BUCK

Why cant you come with me tomorrow?

MILO

Tomorrow's Saturday, that's my gig with the Montauk train, Ole 38, Montauk and back

SLIM

I'll be on the local to Huntington

VICKI

You want em soft or hard?

MILO

Anyway you like baby, I'll be hard you be soft

BUCK

What's happened to that model that was gonna have her picture taken by Filipino we saw last week?

TOMMY

Which one was that?

MILO

Oh I ran into that Chinee girl, I havent seen her since

TOMMY

What Chinee girl?

MILO

She got my victrola, she just got everthing, "Wee Small Hours" and my Webcor three-speed box . . . . . Man, I shouldna done it, aaff

JULE

I'll make the run?

BUCK

Will you?

TOMMY

Go, man, go, I'll have a blast . . .

MILO

(SINGING) Fine day, fine day, I can see this is gonna be my lucky day, I have this dog-eared brakie here from El Paso Texas six foot six and lookin down on me from the upper heights of the cold mountains so tied up in his long suspenders, fat chances outa one that Slim you're sunk, pal

SLIM

Guess I am

MILO

Got you cornered, boy, got you cornered . . . Now you cant make a move outa there . . . . . there is one move you could do but I aint gonna tell you what it is, natcherly, and I reckon you could figure it out in a while but I aint gonna tell you what it is

BUCK

Neal wins the world series? the first game of the world series? What about that bishop over there

MILO

Huh? what bishop

BUCK

Yeah, it is a checkmate

MILO

Checkmate indeed

JULE

That's the way the ball bounces

MILO

(SWEEPING THE CHESSES OFF THE BOARD) We're ORF!

SLIM

Now wait, wait wait a minute, wait a minute, put em back where you had em, I had an idea, I wasnt checkmate there . . . . For one thing you can put that knight over there to show me the position, you didnt put it back but I could see it—if the knight was back there . . . . where was it, put it back there

MILO

Here?

SLIM

No no, on the other side . . . er, it was closer . . . it was a black check knight, the bishop was there

MILO

The bishop was there?

SLIM

The bishop wasn't there?

BUCK

How can you tell now?

MILO

We're ORF to the races and it's Lazy Charley taking the lead (AND HERE MILO STARTS TO PUT THE CHESSES AWAY IN HIS POCKET IN THE BOX) at the clubhouse turn there's your—darling marvelous eggs just fluffy and light (AS THE GIRL BRINGS THE EGGS) hm just like my baby's puddin, hoo! . . . . and now listen now old Buck now old wild sonumbitch dont you get drunk today on that w-i-n-e cause boy, we've got—who's got a cigarette, I'm fresh out—we've got to go out there, and we've got something to do *today*

BUCK

Finish up that fifth, Jule

JULE

Here

BUCK

Okay, some left

JULE

You better drink, you better drink, you better drink (SINGING) . . . hum . . . and it's Oh the greatest, the greatest, the greatest . . .

(JULE GOES OUT, CLOSES THE DOOR, HE'S GOING OUT TO GET THE WINE)

MILO

Butter, butter! where's the butter! Aint there no bread around here? Aint there no Follies Girls or anything? Have to run out there in the Olympic Series and do the standing broad jump all by myself . . . . looking for your eyes I was, in Akron, for a glimpse of your eyes . . . . . .

SLIM

I'll take this piece of butter . . . . I'll take this piece here and butter it up real careful, and eat it real slow, I'll eat this side on the plate

MILO

Dont you invade my territory while I eat on this side, except for a little bit of yellow there, pal

SLIM

Well you can have that yellow but I'll take that cookie

MILO

What cookie! Ack, ow, you dawg, snap! . . . . Now boys we're short on time (LOOKS AT HIS WATCH) . . . How's your old timepiece there Slim . . . . short on time.

(THEY BOTH LOOK AT THEIR WATCHES) Your timepiece there's alright?

SLIM

I see forty-two

MILO

I got forty one and one half . . . . dammit . . . . forty one and three quarters . . . . . who's right and who's wrong . . . . . Coffee ah coffee, slurp, good old hot holy way-I-like-it telling you, Tommy, coffee, you just washin your river underwear when you're tryin to figure out them horses, you're wastin your time, boy, I'm tellin you about Lazy Charley, he's *right*

TOMMY

Listen man, I've been playin the horses since before you were born, remember that, I'm much older than you are

BUCK

Did you ever hear that story about the time Tommy and Denis played the horses, Milo, Tommy had to deliver a Buddha statue to Riverside Drive in some kind of seabag and wanted to make the daily double and so he rushed, after he delivered he rushed to the racetrack on time and there's Denis up in the clubhouse with some fancy dolls and they see this little guy rushing through the crowd with this big empty bag on his back and the girl turns to him and she says "What's Tommy doing with that *huge* bag?" and Denis says "Tommy's got the horses figured out so well today he thought he'd bring a big bag"

MILO

Mdah

BUCK

And the girl believed it

SLIM

A big bag to put all his money in, huh?

BUCK

And the girl believed it

TOMMY

Wasnt exactly like *that*

MILO

More butter? Okay then it's mine . . . . hup whoop, now wait a second here what the hell do you mean about time? now it's forty three isnt it . . . . for krissakes all I hear is talk about Time and God around here . . . . Yass sir . . . . Havent had so much in there, nice front, nice side, nice hippies, flippy dippy

TOMMY

Who's that?

MILO

Well I'm lookin at a picture in the paper here, flippy dippy, that's the way I figure it myself, shooting star of mercy shoulda had a bleak face, heh?

BUCK

There's another one, O is she a gone cutie though aint she (LOOKING OVER MILO'S SHOULDER AT THE PAPER)

MILO

Where where?

BUCK

She's gone

MILO

Oh *man*, let's eat . . . . let's eat . . . and now (STRETCHING) ah now . . . children . . . . this foolishness is . . . . short on time, it's forty three and a half now men we're ready to go?

BUCK

What about Jule?

MILO

Well he's not coming to the racetrack, now I've got exactly twenty eight minutes to make that on-duty, and there's a sweet little baby pussy I want you to see on the way, goin to give us exactly or maybe less than that, *clean*, about, ooh I dont know, about, if she's in, we'll have maybe we'll have one minute (DROPS ASHTRAY ON THE FLOOR, PICKS IT UP) . . . . Er but boys, stayin around in Jule Chauncey's kitchen here, we're being *ostracized* here, we gotta get on down the line there . . . . Yes sir, we're ready to roll? Hm, and, hey look at this one here, that's some nice little sweet sumpin, do you hear that—dig that little dress? now all on account of this *Manuel* ideas of yours, Buck, the cat you want us to go to the racetrack of yours, Buck, the cat you want us to go to the racetrack with, now we're gonna be late for the racetrack and we gotta—

BUCK

Manuel's a great guy

MILO

I mean . . . we cant see the little girl if we have to go get *him*

BUCK

I promise you, I know

MILO

Well, *man*

BUCK

Why dont you like him?

MILO

He's one of those guys, you know dont do you no good

BUCK

Why? they got em rough and mean, but Manuel's a great poet, a great kid

MILO

Wiggle though that as you will but I dont understand him

BUCK

Why, because he keeps yelling in a loud voice? that's the way he talks

MILO

Not that . . . . just, man dont you know me, I know, I've known him—but—

BUCK

Ah he's a good kid, he's no—he's our *friend*

MILO

The friend's so-si-e-tay

BUCK

Alright

MILO

I see here that we now have . . . . where did all those guys go? . . . . . Eh, you can sit here and I'll sit over here, then we'll go down we'll go see my baby pussy and we're gonna go get M-a-n-u-e-l to go to the racetrack with us and we have just enough time Tommy to have a little—but now wait a minute now . . . . we do have three minutes, two and a half at the most, now what we've got to have is another picolo for Buck—now wait a minute

TOMMY

I got one here

MILO

Well you've got one, now here's—we're gonna have a trio, did I ever tell you that one about the—There once was a man from Canute (THEY TAKE OUT THEIR FLUTES), had warts on his cheroot, he poured acid on these, and now when he pees, he fingers his cheroot like a flute? D'I ever tell you that

(EVERYBODY LAUGHING AND HIGH)

Never heard that one? We gotta, also we can hear the trio, and we'll trade off—Now you'll play the white picolo, Buck you play the black picolo, I'll play the sweetpotato for one minute and then you'll take the sweetpotato we'll pass it around in rotation see so we dont get on any bum kicks because of the poor instrument. *Sit down*! sit down to the quartet, the Beethov—come on, string quartet man–this is a clarinet trio, you unnerstand (EXPERIMENTAL FLUTINGS)

TOMMY

Who's gonna pass on his ability here

MILO

On ability Vicki herself will pass on

TOMMY

Is she listening?

MILO

No, we dont, no we just want a three-way here . . .

TOMMY

A little cooperation here

(SLIM DRUMS ON INVERTED SAUCEPAN)

MILO

Listen, for real tea-head goof kicks, man, you cant have any—we gotta be like a string quartet, no beat and syncopation whatsoever, see, and we'll just goof you unnerstand, like a string quartet, you unnerstand, but he'll play his solo there, you know like he just did, drum solo, see—Let's make sure we're getting everything here (ADJUSTS CHAIR TO FACE VICKI . . . FIRST NOTES, CHALLENGES OF FLUTES)

Hey, man, the guy who has the soft one must be sure and get his thing to hear close enough so Vicki can hear

TOMMY

I cant hear my thing . . .

MILO

No yours can be heard, yours is the loudest, you sit like this, and Buck's about right, he might turn that way a little, but I have to keep turning that way . . . . Now let's goof again, let's goof again (LAUGHING TITTERING MANIACALLY), I didn't mean to interrupt and all this 'cause you guys . . . . .

BUCK

Well as you say it all goes down the same hole

TOMMY

Hey I got to get a girl to give me incentive

MILO

(FLUTING) That was, ah, that was amazing, I began to think of snake charmers and then I began to think of the, toot toot toot, and so therefore I had to cut you all a great mighty solo, my mighty solo was about to come in there

TOMMY

Oh, the rape charmers!

MILO

Ready?
(ANNOUNCING:) The rape charmers of the Indian Plantation System. . . .

(ALL THREE PLAY, AS SLIM LISTENS IN THE SAUCEPAN)

Clarity of tone!

TOMMY

Ah!

MILO

An attribute

TOMMY

Yes Sahib

(THEY PLAY)

MILO

Slowly, children, slowly (THEY PLAY SLOWLY) Now we trade! now we trade!

(GRABBING TOMMY'S PICOLO)

TOMMY

Hey!

MILO

We gotta get accustomed to all the instruments

TOMMY

Hey geez hey

MILO

No, like we—hee hee—come on go on, music, there you are (HANDING SWEETPOTATO TO TOMMY)

TOMMY

What is the hole here?

MILO

That's it, see

TOMMY

Hey what's this little tiny hole here? this isnt a—what kinda hole is that hey!

MILO

Never seen a hole that small before

TOMMY

Is this the small hole?

MILO

It's the small hole, the mighty seven holes and the mighty seven epistles

(TOMMY BLOWS)

All wind . . . all hollow blowing . . . . The hole's up here . . . There you are

SLIM

Hey Milo, short on time!

MILO

Hup hup (PICKS UP CHESSBOARD, CHESSMEN, BIBLE, RACING FORM) Here we go men!

BUCK

So long Vicki, so long, see you later. Short on time

VICKI

What?

BUCK

Short on time!

(AND THEY RUSH OUT. AND AFTER ABOUT TEN SECONDS THE GIRL SITS IN THE CHAIR AND PUTS HER HEAD IN HER HANDS AND LAUGHS ..... AND THEN THE DOOR OPENS AND JULE HER HUSBAND WALKS IN)

VICKI

(LOOKING UP) Milo was short on time

JULE

Short on *time*! .... You know what Buck said ...

VICKI

... you want to?

JULE

—kiss her *belly*! Sure, I'll see what I can do about giving you a smack of H today .... And now I'm gonna have a glass of wine. ... How many sands are there, to be removed from the Pacific Ocean, each time you pour a million gallons of joy juice into the emptiness of all space, and does it even matter. (DRINKS)

ACT TWO

SCENE ONE

(FIRST RACE . . . . . ARM IN ARM, MILO IN THE MIDDLE, WEARING FULL BRAKEMAN'S UNIFORM'S GOT BOTH ARMS AROUND BUCK AND THE NEW CAT MANUEL AND MANUEL'S SAYING:)

MANUEL

Yay you guys, wow, you told me you'd get me at twelve o'clock sharp and you were half an hour late . . .

MILO

Midnight

MANUEL

Mid-night? you told me damn you, that you was gonna be—yah I know you, I know it's all plots, everywhere it's plots, everybody wants to hit me over the head and deliver my body to the tomb! . . . . . . The last time I had a dream about truth it was you, it was you, it was you two, and it was much more with golden birds, though, and all sweet fawns consoled me, I was the Consoler, I lifted my skirts of Divinity to all the little children who trudged by, I changed into Pan, I piped them sweet green tune, right under a tree, and you were that tree . . . Milo you were that tree! I see it all now, you cant follow me!

MILO

Well, ah, that's perfectly alright my boy, it's that breach of time when you see a pedestrian or a car or an upcoming crackup just crack right on up, nothin's going to happen, if it dont separate you got that extry breach of time to sure give em grace but ordinarily ten times outa one boy them astral bodies separate cat and that's because it's all figured out in the hall up there where they make the cee-ga-ree-los!

MANUEL

Ach! Milo I cant stand you, you, you give me nothing but bull, he pulls my ears, it'll never end, I quit, I give up—what time is the first race, man? here we are!

BUCK

Manuel's a razzer! Manuel the Razzer! One of them guys likes to razz the boys, you know

MILO

The time of the first race is about out of reach now, thanks to all these various developments . . . . Naturally we cant play the daily double

BUCK

Who wants to play the daily double anyway? The odds are never long enough, it's a hundred to one, a fifty to one chance you got pickin two successive winners and all they give you is, like, seven-to-one and all that

MANUEL

Daily double?

MILO

Yes, sir, daily double . . . but speakin about—now—let's get back here now, that horse, now I'll tell you now, that this—ah, and so, I was telling you, the third choice horse paid six dollars to show yesterday, three to five dollars, and he paid five dollars to show twice, and then four three times, a little under four, about twenty forty cents, *twice,* came in the money all day first second and third *all day,* now you realize what that means?

MANUEL

Numbers! numbers!

MILO

Now, let's, you, here we are at the racetrack now, let's not, now what we should do and inasmuch as you dont believe me both of you, I beg you to see and to understand—I'll tell you what I'll—I'll play win all day, according to Lazy Charley's System, third choice—Now Lazy Charley, now you realize Manuel he was an old hand at bettin that system and when he died they found him dead at the race-track right in that clubhouse there, forty thousand dollars worth of uncashed tickets in his chest, which means that by that time he was plankin real heavy and affectin the odds himself, why God just yanked him right out of this earth because he was gonna upset it

MANUEL

But I've only got three dollars!

MILO

This'll come in time . . .

(AND HE REMOVES HIS ARMS FROM AROUND THE TWO FELLOWS)

Boy when I get really rollin I'm gonna start building

monasteries and Samsarean retreats and hand out five-dollar bills to deserving bums in skid row and in fact even people in trolleys then I get me a Mercedes Benz boy and just go spinning down to Mexico City on that El Paso Highway doing 165 on the straightaways and boy you *know* that's gotta be in low gear 'cause when you come to that curve you gotta make it at 80 or a hundred and it's gotta swash that car through it's a matter of sideswiping that curve with your *brakes, yes sir*! Now what we'll do, I'll play to win, Manuel play to place, Buck play to show, all day on the third choice

BUCK

I havent got no money, I've got 35 cents . . . . I aint gonna *bet*, I aint got no money . . . . . Let's get a beer, somebody buy me a beer . . . . . It's beer and baseball and hotdogs

MILO

Now just a minute here boy, now third choice in the betting means I'm gonna bet on, ah—

MANUEL

I'm gonna bet on number nine! It's a mystical number! It's Dante's mystical number!

MILO

Nine? Nine? Why that dog's goin off at thirty-to-one . . . .

Now look here, old buddy, see here we are at the racetrack, and there's your flags flyin on the flagpoles and here she is the bugle call, now we're alone now and we're all set and I've got a chance to really talk to you fellas and tell you a few things, I want you to *know* how to win at the races

BUCK

How's your horse running, your third choice in the 2nd race?

MILO

Where? what? right now she's number six, you see, 'course all that can change as the bottom of the hat

BUCK

What was that you wanted to tell me about when we got out of the train?

MILO

I'm feelin so fine, Buck, Manuel, I'm feelin *so* good on this great afternoon . . . . here we are and we're gonna make some money and talk—cant you hide that bottle better there boy—we're gonna—

BUCK

It's only a poorboy, it's almost finished . . . . here, there, I'll finish it and throw it in the wastebasket

MILO

That's right, I'm gonna buy you a beer . . .

BUCK

We'll be respectable drinkin outa cartons, won't we

MILO

That's right, ole daddy, and now *tonight*, this is after we do all this bettin and winnin here—

BUCK

Hey look, look at the toteboard, he's changed to seven!

MILO

That's right, seven it is, seven times seven is forty nine times my brother's been hurt, we'll just stand here by the window real close and sneak in that line when the warning buzzer rings, now Mannie you come along

BUCK

How much have you lost in the last two days?

MILO

Last two days, man I'm five thousand in the hole now

BUCK

Five *thousand*! is that all that money you got for breaking your rib? What's . . . the wife sayin?

MILO

Aw naturally she doesnt know about it and I dont want you to tell her about it, I got my baby pudding in mah pocket right here, I got joy in my backpocket

BUCK

Alright, let me see it

MILO

She's in, it's over there, it's over there, it's over there

BUCK

Look, Milo, there's a new flash, you know I hope it stays seven because you know that kid is a good rider, Valenzuala, that little Mexican cat boy he really can drive a horse, dammit, what strong wrists those little guys have . . . you know when I was a kid I used to go to the racetrack with my father and my—

MILO

That's alright my boy, now listen now, we're gonna wait at the beer counter here and as the bettors merge into long panicky lines waiting as the horses near the six furlong pole and the buzzer's gonna go, you know, and they all hustle and push and line up and so on, we just wait till the last minute cool and collected like old Lazy Charley, nobody's even once gonna look out at the actual horses but we're gonna know all about the numbers, you see, them astral numbers . . . . Now you can have the cigar smoke and shuffling feet, yah

BUCK

Hey look over here, over that crowd, over that field, and that distant Jamaica gastank across the roofs far away, it's Jamaica Racetrack Long Island New York but it's definitely an ant heap in Nirvana, aint it . . . . . . Those cars out there on that little highway are smaller than I can believe, it's a . . . . space trick! And look at those jockeys!

MILO

Alright boys, now we're gonna line up here, as soon as we finish this beer . . . But I'm worried about that dog 6, in spite of Lazy Charley's System, Matchstick, you know, beat Burning Bush here last Tuesday, I dont like it . . .

BUCK

How do you know you dont like it?

MILO

Ah well I was looking at Tommy's form here

BUCK

What do you have to worry about, just bet on third choice, Lazy Charley's System, that's all

MILO

Well that's what I'm trying to tell you—

(MEANWHILE MILO IS LOOKING VERY NEAT AND CLEAN, IT'S THE FIRST RACE, AND EVERYBODY IS VERY CLEANLY DRESSED AND THERE'S NO LITTER ON THE FLOOR OF THE STAGE, EVERYBODY LOOKS VERY HAPPY, THEY'RE ALL LINED UP, EVERYBODY'S TALKING)

Now Buck damn you I'm trying to tell you, to stick to the third choice? sure! I wouldnt be five thousand in the hole if I had, that's why I wanted you to come with me today Buck and make me stick to the line

BUCK

Alright, Milo, I'll see to it that you stick to your system

MILO

That's right, Buck now you get it that way, that's the whole point and the reason why I'm bringing you is that you've got to make me stick to it

BUCK

That's right, I know what the matter with you—

MILO

That's right, I'm worried about that dog 10, that's Candle Heart boy, he can go a mile in one thirty six, he's been running in high company around here lately too

BUCK

Yeah but that's alright, but that's not your system

MILO

Exactly m'boy, m'friend, exactly, we just go ahead and forget all about him dont we

BUCK

That's right

MANUEL

I'm gonna bet on number nine! I have a feeling and a vision about Number Nine! It's Dante's mystical number!

MILO

Now that's what I need is a little sense here, makes me stick to my system . . . . I dont know why we brought this here *Manuel* (ASIDE TO BUCK)

BUCK

That's right, my boy

(AND MILO PUTS HIS ARM AROUND BOTH OF THEM, HAVING FINISHED HIS BEER, AND SAYS:)

MILO

Now the whole point of the whole thing is I've got to get that five thousand dollars back so I can have some operation capital here you see 'cause I raise the ante up to fifty or a hundred a race and pretty soon boy I'll be plankin in my imaginary hotter-than-Charley-prophecy that's when it'd start really makin the money—Hey how's the back of my coat? here's the brush, you mind brushing it off, for specks, any specks on the back of my coat?

BUCK

Few

MILO

Brush it (BUCK BRUSHES) That's fine good buddy, now let's see, here's a cigarette here to keep our hands contained—any specks on my shoes? how's that old handkerchief of yours, come on down there and get down on your knees and brush them old black railroad shoes boy, I gotta look clean here, now it's clear as day I see from the toteboard here seven's gonna run off at third choice, that's our horse, right?

BUCK

Naturally

MANUEL

I'm gonna play nine!

MILO

Manuel, what you should do is play the horse that I play all day in every one of the next seven races, but play it to place, because you see 6 is a mad dog and 10 can fly man, I've seen that dumb jockey there that's gonna ride him today fall off of him two weeks ago and he took off and came home alone by ten lengths that horse without a rider . . . . you see, but I have dreams too, you know, Manuel, speaking of your mystical numbers

MANUEL

Dreams?

MILO

Yeah just as a little side issue today and before we go and plank our bets now and since they're gonna be ringing the buzzer soon I'll tell you, and since I just got paid yesterday you see man now listen I had a dream that this gone little jockey cat Pulido, you know Pulido that guy you dug down in the paddock there Buck that while back, why, he—

BUCK

You mean the jockey that's gonna ride number nine, Manuel's horse, he was nice to the owner's little son, I remember him the other day, a real nice Mexican kid, sits on the horse digging the audience as he rides by the stands

MILO

Yeah he's on a—Oh, in my dream in an old engyne going around the track but going the wrong way, see, way out in front and in my dream the race is going from the clubhouse turn up here to the head of the stretch goin backwards and what happens but bam, just as they hit the win-wire going the wrong way he's ahead and the whole gol-dang train blows up, that's right men, explodes and Pulido is over the wire all by himself!

BUCK

Man, he really won that race!

MILO

Exactly, exactly, what's what I'm trying to tell you, and seeing all how I got my pay yesterday I thought just for the hell of it today I'd plant a little bit side bet on Pulido in every race

BUCK

But that's not sticking to your Charley System

MILO

Since . . . that . . . dream . . . evidently . . . . presupposes . . . . dont you think, Manuel, that he might run three four maybe five mounts or even two, bring em in straight at any kind of price? and he's riding . . . he's riding . . . he's riding *nine*! That's Manuel's horse and dig the name, man, the name of the horse, *The Driver*! see that's the dream

BUCK

But that's not following your system!

MILO

But as I say it was an extryspecial day, now you've got to admit yourself, Buck—

BUCK

Now wait a minute . . . . If you dont follow your system, what are you gonna do? How long have you been losing five thousand dollars?

MILO

No, nothing, ah, nothing, ah—this is just the first dream I had, 'course baby you see I have dreams all the time, I loses money, and nobody has any money, dass iss the way it goes . . . . .

BUCK

Yeah

MILO

And disincarnate entities, I go to the betting window, like I told you I got my third choice, say it's Number One, I go up and just as I'm about to say "ten dollars to win on Number One" I hear a voice say *Number Ten*! I come out there with a ticket on Number Ten!

BUCK

Yah yah yah yah yah yah yah yah

MILO

Spirits of course, hopin around waitin to possess a human body soon as possible so's to get that invaluable opportunity as you know and you told me yourself about how slim the chances are of being reborn a human being, that gone turtle that swims out into infinite seas throughout eternity and comes up once in a while and sticks his head up—

BUCK

Yeah, the floating noose—

MILO

—floating noose as Buddha say, what are the chances of that turtle coming up just when the noose is over his head? trillion to one? What long odds! You see this is our chance of being reborn a human being so as to work out the previous chance, maybe we have to lose and suffer a little bit in this world so I'm gonna play a little side bet on that dream jockey and I'm gonna play my third choice which apparently's gonna be Number Six now so I'm gonna go over the window now . . . . And the air is filled with disks, aint it, look at the disks and flying saucers up there

MANUEL

Where?

BUCK

This very racetrack which I can see from looking at it now far across the infield, see the little cars going down the old shore,—ant heap in Heaven

MILO

And so ants, and friends, how do I know that there isnt some friendly entity wants to tell me the winner . . . . . man when I hear those voices I just dont care, I mean I really hear those voices and I got to pay attention to them

BUCK

Supposing that they were *evil* entities trying to make you lose since you're so certain that the third choice system was revealed to you to redact your karma, see, bring it back!

MILO

Man I'm telling you, I dont—listen, now—(THE WARNING BUZZER RINGS) There she is now, look, seven is third choice now, switched the last minute—Just as clear cut third choice's I've ever seen—Dammit have you got an old handkerchief I can—?—wait a minute, alright—

BUCK

Look here's a program! (PICKING ONE UP ON THE GROUND)

MILO

Good, no sense wasting a quarter on them damn things

BUCK

Buy me another beer when they're off huh as soon as you've placed the bet

MILO

Man I have exactly twenty one 10-dollar bills, that's for eight races—

BUCK

Well alright

MILO

—seven . . . I dont wanta change—I dont wanta get hungup on change and be short sixty cents and not be able to play that full potential percentage man in the eighth race, it's got to come

BUCK

Manuel can you buy me a beer?

MANUEL

Sure, man

MILO

You wait right here, fellas

MANUEL

I'm goin with you!

MILO

That's alright I'll be right back

(SO MANUEL AND MILO GO TO THE PLACING WINDOW AND THEY PLACE THEIR BETS AND COME BACK TOGETHER)

BUCK

Who'd you bet?

MILO

Third choice of course

BUCK

But you've got three tickets there, let me see

MILO

Four

BUCK

Four tickets?

MILO

Well you see I figured out that this dream jockey and then my third choice Lazy Charley and I was worried about that dog 10 and that other dog 6 . . . . .

BUCK

Put no stock in dreams and omens, Oh *man*! . . . .

MILO

I just put a little side bet on that dog that Tommy was talking about, I knew he was going to cause trouble

BUCK

Alright, alright . . . . how can you follow Lazy Charley's System, you wont make any profit this way if you're going to make any at all

MILO

That's the way it's been all along, man

BUCK

Well that's how you've been losing five thousand dollars, why dont you control yourself!

MILO

(WHISPERING) That's what I was trying—the next race—oh look at Manuel there, he's just coming back with his ticket there, number 9

BUCK

But Milo you brought me here to make you stick to your system!

MILO

That's right old buddy and you've been doing very well!

BUCK

I aint been doing so good, you're sort of—why are you so resigned about your own madness!

MILO

Every night I pray that I'll stick to that third choice, I'll tell you that much

BUCK

Well by God, I dont know—

(AND THE RACE IS RUN, "THEY'RE OFF!" "AND IT'S BURNING BUSH TAKING THE LEAD, AND" . . ALL THAT STUFF, AND YOU KNOW THE WAY A RACE)

MILO

There I told ya!

(AND ITS NOODLES SECOND BY A LENGTH," AND ALL THE VARIOUS HORSES):

Pulido! Pulido! My dream jockey'll do it!

("HALFMILE POLE, IT'S THE HALFMILE POLE," AND SO ON SO THE RACE IS RUN AND YOU GET ALL THAT STUFF ON THE STAGE, AND SO:)

BUCK

Well Milo, that horse of yours they'll be bringin him by lamplight in my dreams

MILO

Good! When third choice comes in third naturally that's as it should be, right? seein as how he was third choice he should third-choice it to the public's satisfaction, good God man just let him lose *all* he wants, the more he loses the stronger I get, because the percentage is on my side after *that*

BUCK

And what about your number nine, Manuel?

MANUEL

(IN ASTONISHMENT) How's that?

MILO

Listen, as the third choice repeatedly uses my bets increase, so that when he does come in I gain by the large bit, *back*, all I lost, and gain *more*

BUCK

It's all in the numbers

MANUEL

It's amazing, some mysteries number should come to me again, probably nine again, it's like roulette, the gambler, you know Dolgoruky kept putting all he had on one thing, and broke the house, and I shall be like Dolgoruky, I dont care . . . . . You see Milo, Buck, if I lose it's because I'm a bum, and if I'm a—it's because I'm crap, and if I'm crap it's because the moon shines on crap! Shine on crap! Eat my babies! . . . . Because you know every day a poem creeps up into my mind and it becomes a high poem, that's just the way I say it . . . . .

MILO

Alright, alright, poetry, poetry, pickles in a barrell, boys we gotta make some money here today now . . . . This aint getting us nowhere here . . . . *that* dog . . . .

(AT THIS MOMENT AN OLD WOMAN COMES UP TO THE THREE MEN IN THE PLAY, SHE HAS BIG BLANK BLUE EYES AND SPINSTERISH IN FACT TIGHT*BUNNED PIONEER HAIR, SHE LOOKS LIKE A GRANT WOOD PORTRAIT, YOU EXPECT TO SEE GOTHIC BARNS IN BACK OF HER, SINCERE AS ALL GET-OUT . . . SAYS TO MILO:)

WOMAN

Hey there Milo, bet on three and if you give me half, I have no money, huh? just bet two dollars and if you win give me half

MILO

You mean 3 in the third race? that dog, he wont win

MANUEL

What is he? what is she? All these *mad* people around here!

MILO

Ah man (LAUGHING, AS SHE GOES AWAY), I've known her for a long time . . . . I used to borrow money from *her* . . . . . See I bring all these people here on this racetrack train and I have to have certain relations with them, and, ah, I did get a few bets outa her one time and that little crippled newsboy there . . . . See after the eighth race we gotta run like hell outa here and get back on that train so I can give the sign to the engineer and we go back to New York—Now this here third race here, you see of course seventh choice often comes in twice a day and, ah—

MANUEL

(LOOKING AROUND) What are all these *mad* people?

MILO

You see, Manuel, if you want to win some money today you better follow *me*, now, never mind your mystical numbers, now the obvious horse in this third race clear and clean-cut a third choice as I've ever seen all alone in there at six-to-one, is Old Number Ten! . . .

MANUEL

Number *Two*! *That's* my favorite number!

MILO

Number two, not only is he a dog but that jockey that's ridin him keeps fallin *off!*

BUCK

Yeah . . . I myself keep scanning this program which I finally appropriated off the ground for strange hints like this horse here Classic Face sired by Manuel Champion and his dam is Erwina, or I look for stranger hints like Grandpa Buck! or The Dreamer! . . . Here's one, that's weird, Night Clink, heh heh, which must mean the time I was in the clink or sumpin . . . . You could think of a million bets you could make . . . . . The way we're going now we'll just end up just sittin in benches in the upper grandstand and wont be able to see the starting gate, you know it's right down there, I wanta go on the fence man, Let's go down the fence so I can explain to Manuel about how the horses—the starter in his box, how he presses the button that rings the bell bats open the bat-cages and out they lunge, man, watch those jockeys, everyone of them has got a hand of steel battin away on the horses .... Like Johnny Longden, he's older than the three of us put together! Ah, and things like that you're missing.

MANUEL

Number Two is my favorite number! Or either that or I'll go back to Number Nine

MILO

Folly the system, man! I'm pleading with you! I told you about Lazy Charley, how they found him dead with forty five thousand dollars worth of uncashed win tickets—

BUCK

Listen Manuel, Lazy Charley just sat around you know sippin coffee between races, and wearing a pince-nez probably, and came out at last minute odds and saw the score and went out and made his bet and maybe went to the head a little bit, it's all in the numbers, the third choice, the concensus of the multitude reduced to a third degree which has been mathematically figured to come in as many percent times so it just keeps givin you bits accordin to the losses you've suffered, you're bound to win, or bored, unless a tragic streak of lustres, or losses—

MILO

That's right, tragic! Now listen to Buck, Manuel, and you'll make some money!

MANUEL

Okay, okay, but I wanta play Number 2 too in this race because it's my lucky number . . . . . Look at those horses, they have such skinny legs, they can get hurt. Hah? they can get hurt . . . .

BUCK

Yeah . . . . .

ACT TWO

SCENE TWO

(NOW IT'S THE EIGHTH RACE, EVERYBODY'S DISSHEVELED, MILO'S REMOVED HIS BLUE BRAKEMAN'S HAT, BLUE COAT, JUST IN SHIRTSLEEVES, SLEEVES ROLLED UP, UNDONE COLLAR, NO NECKTIE, MANUEL'S DISSHEVELED, EVERY*BODY'S DISSHEVELED, THEY'RE STANDING THERE:)

BUCK

Yeah . . . . see?

MILO

Now meanwhile—

BUCK

So what were you talking about, back there, when we got out of the train again?

MILO

Give me a cigarette, I'm all out . . . . Wal, I was just sayin, it used to not feel couple years ago that it was hardly worth it to complete the sentence and it got so try as I might I couldnt, that's what I'm sayin, but I'm tryin to tell you now, see, Edgar Cayce did get all his powers from one tremendous ordeal in a previous lifetime when he was a Roman Soldier, and was left mortally wounded with a big spear in his back, man, on a plain, nobody to help him, took three days for him to die and during those three days he learned how to withstand pain and content his mind and face the patient death, see it's like the Bishop says that we're gonna see tonight, the million words that he uses, longsuffering patience . . . . Oh, we had, now, together with them other words that he uses, like sincerity of heart, and so as you think for instance and but—Hey, here comes sumpin . . .

(A BLONDE PASSES)

BUCK

Yeah—How long do these rebirths go on? When are you gonna lend me that book?

MILO

Just as long as there's somethin like that walking around . . .

BUCK

Why doesnt God just dont step in and stop the world with a snap of his finger?

MILO

We'll just amble on over there and stand next to her, huh? Man let's go, Manuel come on, you're the one with the words, she's got a friend I see . . . . see the brunette friend? Dig those little tight-fittin skirts man, and besides now, come on now to get back! now you've been saying all day long boy that we're in Heaven now havent you Buck boy?

BUCK

Yessir that's what I said, that's what I saw

MILO

Lemme see that program!

BUCK

(STANDING HUNCHED HANDS IN POCKETS) Well, last race comin up, sun goin down

MILO

Now, two minutes till post time, looks like Number 7 at this moment

BUCK

The Cossack isnt it, a good jockey, Longden. You know why I like Longden? He won a stake race one time and I was down by the judges' stand and I didnt know who won the race, what jockey, they were all covered with mud that time. There's nothin there but a gang of women who were there with a big silver cup to receive the winner, and I saw old John Longden suddenly standing *shorter* than all the other jockeys in the winner's circle, 50 years old riding against 20 year old kids, man I cried, I remember Johnny Longden trottin across the road in Rockingham 25 years ago, with Jimmy Stout, who's dead now. See, the soul of Jimmy Stout's gone, ... where has it gone Milo?

MILO

Out there, man, and if he didnt have fulfilled his karma you know damn well he's trottin right up there tryin to get back right here in this racetrack to atone for his sins in the name of Jesus Christ boy

MANUEL

Wow you guys, why dont you concentrate on the betting! Here we've been taking trips to the men's room and the beer counter and the coffee counter and hotdogs and finally when the last race is coming up here we are, these characters of the track that looked so confident in the first race, look at them now, man! they're all looking for money in the ground, they aint gonna find it there! Just like the thrashing doves in Chinatown, there's no hope, they have their necks cut! I dont wanta live in a world like this! And there he is, now, running around and they're looking for *women* and they're going to take them home or something, *man* .... We oughta take separate leaks—Let's go back to the sweet city! I keep getting the feeling that as Milo wins he really loses and as he loses he really wins, it's all ephemeral, it can't be grabbed by the hand, it's *hurt*! The *money* can be grabbed by the hand, I wanted to buy myself a new typewriter with the money I put in but look! there's no patience in eternity! eternity! meaning more than all time and beyond all that little crap and forever! Milo you cant win, you cant lose, all is ephemeral, all is hurt! These are my feelings! I'm a sly gambler . . . but I wont gamble on *Heaven*! That's the exact amount of teaching Christ gave me! or Buddha! or Mohammed! or the Torah! Even if he ends up with a highly successful day, every horse comes in the money and you win you'll turn around and you say "Buck you sonumbitch if you'd a squeezed two little measly dollars out of those jeans each race and done what I said you'd have a nice fifty dollar bill tonight." What would Buck with a fifty dollar bill, all he wants is 35 cents! But it's one of your happy days,

I can see that. I can see you folding your money all proud in neat little arrangements with the small bills on the outside in your pocket. We'll come walking out of this racetrack and pass the parkinglot where your little car is parked by a railroad track and I'll say "There's your parking-place, you just park there every day" and you know what you'll say to me Milo? you'll say "Yes me boy and besides there'll be a Mercedes Benz in the place of that thing there in a few years." It's a big lake a dreams! . . . . . .

MILO

Let's place the bets, it's the Angel Gabriel just made a speech and Archangel Michael is standing behind us, see how tall he is?

BUCK

Yeh, man. How's she looking now?

MILO

Who, the Archangel? er, still one . . . . . Changed from seven to one, the favorite is even money, second choice is five-to-two and he's all by himself at six-to-one . . . . . How much you s'sposed to put on him now, did you figure that out on the pencil there?

BUCK

According to Lazy Charley it's 45 dollars but I've got this

figured that you've got to save a little bit of that for your dream jockey, the dead man, and that worrisome old troublesome other horse you were talking about, (LAUGHS) starting to play the horses wrong with *you* now . . . . Get me another beer will ya?

MILO

Wait here, I'll get you a beer

BUCK

Dont *bet* too much, I'll go in line with ya

MILO

That's alright, now Buck, that's alright, 'cause tonight we're gonna go to Huntington, we're gonna go to my pad, hear the Bishop speak, drive home in two cars, his and mine, he's bringing his two aunts you know, as I told you—

BUCK

Yeh

MILO

And, ah, man, wait'll you see him, young cat only 28 like I said a big long black—why he speaks with his eyes *closed*, you know, every now and then he looks a little bit at the congregation sittin there in those benches and they're all quiet, you can hear their bellies rumble, sometimes he trembles, lets loose long big Indian songs, sermons and—why shit, the wife knows all that, she sends—he sends her pamphlets and all that stuff . . . and . . .

BUCK

Manuel, what about *your* pamphlet?

MANUEL

I have a leaf in my pamphlet

MILO

That cat

BUCK

(LAUGHS) Always bettin on number nine because it's Dante's mystical number, say, he even says if he wins he'll buy himself a typewriter so he can write more poems

MILO

Yeah . . . what about, what about if I put twenty on him?

BUCK

No! Follow your system! Supposed to put 45, or at least forty and five on your bloody pollution there whatever that *dream* jockey . . .

MILO

Well figure it on 40 dollars, one to sit, five on number four to win—

BUCK

Now this is one in-carnate entity that's giving you *this* advice, I'm not *dis*-incarnate . . .

MILO

Alright baby alright

BUCK

And if he loses at least you'll have played your system when you come back tomorrow—

MILO

You'll come back and play it for me—

BUCK

Okay buddy

MILO

—and the only thing for us to do now is sit and wait and man as soon as that race is over we've got to hustle back to that train because boy that *crowd,* I'm on duty you know as soon as all that.

BUCK

Where's the hoghead and fireman that brought the train in, eating lunch in the engyne or what?

MILO

No man, (LAUGHING), they've been playing the horses, haven't you seen them, they're wearing business clothes you know. I come out here in my uniform but they change, you know they dont want people to know that they're playing the horses

BUCK

You mean the whole railroad is going mad?

MILO

Well every day, you know, they put em on this train and they come out and they play money . . .

BUCK

How much do they win a day, sixty-five cents?

MILO

Well, some crippled boys make less . . . . I'll go get your beers (EXITS)

MANUEL

Solid! We'll make it together, Buck, you and me, we'll make it! We'll make it with Milo, we'll make a lot of money and make it on! Even though we havent won today yet I *feel* that we'll win in this eighth race but I *see* you now, I *know* you now, Buck, you're sincere, you really want to win!

BUCK

I dont wanta win. *Milo* wants to win.

MANUEL

Milo! . . I *believe* Milo! . . I *know* he's Jesus Christ's contemporary frightening brother. I just want to—I just dont want to be hung-gup on the wrong *bets,* it's like being hung-gup on the wrong poets, the wrong people, the wrong *side* . . . . .

BUCK

Everything's right side Manuel actually . . .

MANUEL

But maybe I dont *wanta* crash, I dont wanta go to no F-f-f-f-f-french angel, man . . . . *You,* Buck, I see your ideas goin down skid row drunk with the bums, *ach*! I never even thought of doing such a thing, why bring misery on yourself? Let the dog lie. I wanta make money, I dont wanta say "Oh

Ah Ah I've lost my way, Oh Ah Ah Ah I've lost honey, I've lost my way," I havent lost my way yet, I'm a young kid, I'm going to ask the Archangel to let me win . . . . . . Hark! I'll tell the Archangel, the bright herald hears me, I hear his trumpet, (AS MILO RETURNS WITH THE BEERS), . . Hey Milo it's ta ra tara tara tara tara, the bright herald archangel the cat with the long trombone at the start of the race, you dig that?

MILO

Yeah, yes, yes *sir!* yes sir . . . . . There's our boy now (LOOKING OUT), see him out there? That Mexican kid there in the red and white silks? goin down the clubhouse turn? Look at the backs of those horses . . . . . *beautiful* horses! Yes sir . . . . . Mogen David wine, Mogen David wine . . .

BUCK

There's your horse down there!

MILO

Yes *sir*, there he is down there, at the halfmile pole he'll be still ahead by a length and a half and when Wigmo makes his move in second place and Prussia'll be third by a neck, Indian Tale'll be dropped back to third and dead and sunk, Part Tart A Too Tee fifth by a length and Googoo sixth and Stumble trailing the park, come on wham he'll come home straight to daddy and bring me home some honey and butter and stumblebum, now now I can see, can you see . . . . *Man,* he'll make it at the far turn, it's still Wigwam that'll be, you know, down there, but boy when he comes on and that Ishmael start wailin away boy, and comin into the homestretch, and they'll be riding down through you'll hear their little sticks crackin the rumps of those horses and the crowd roar . . . they'll come flashin across that finish line, we'll collect our money . . . we'll—

BUCK

You and Manuel'll run to your little windows and collect your little pittances . . . and what are you gonna do with them, sit in haystack? watch the airplaines? . . .

MILO

We'll be sittin in a airstack and watch the hayplanes, and we'll get our money, and we wont even know what to do with it, huh! fat chance we wont know what to do with it, fat chance *I* wont know what to do with it, I got *expenses,* boy, I got a family, I got a wife and four kids . . . And like you say we'll collect our pittance and we'll get back on that train and bring it back to New York . . . 'Cause boy, no matter what happens, everything that's gonna happen's *bound* to happen, and we're gonna have a *ball*—as long as you feel good in your *gut* . . . . 'cause I *know,* the Lord is on my side

MANUEL

I dont want a world like that from God

BUCK

What do you mean?

MANUEL

That's what I mean, I dont want it. What a way to die!

BUCK

Who's dying

MANUEL

All these creatures, with their necks over barrels, mad people in here . . . If it's all the little doves'll die my eye would have opened a long time ago, I dont like it anyway, I dont *care*

MILO

Manuel get your money out, we're gonna go place the bet now, the warning buzzer's ringing

BUCK

Birds with long sharp knives that shine in the afternoon sun?

MANUEL

Yeah

BUCK

—and old Zing Twing Tong he lives up there in that pad and smokes opium of the world, opiums of Persia? All he's got is a mattress on the floor, a Travler portable radio, and he works, and his works under the mattress? Described as a wretched mean hovel in the New York World Telegram?

MANUEL

Ah Buck you're mad . . . . I'm not gonna think about it, I'm going home and sleep after this, I dont wanta dream about wilted pigs and dead chickens in the barrel and horses and racetracks and no typewriter. .

BUCK

You're right

MANUEL

Besides it's a nowhere movie, we cant go see it, there's no monsters, all it is is a moon man with a suit on, I wanta see monstrous dinosaurs and mammals of the other world! Who wants to pay fifty thousand dollars to see guys with machines and panels and a girl in a monstrous lifebelt skirt! Let's cut out of here after the last race, I'm going *home*

BUCK

All you gotta be, man, is a big sad cloud

MANUEL

I just want classical angels . . . I dont wanta be a big sad cloud

BUCK

Dont you wanta be a giant cloud, that's all I am, a giant cloud, leaning on its side, all vapors, yeah

MANUEL

(SADLY) I wish I was a giant cloud . . .

MILO

Come *on*, man, stop talking about giant clouds and let's go place those bets

(MANUEL AND MILO RUSH OFF)

ACT THREE

(THE SCENE IS A LIVINGROOM OF A RANCH-STYLE HOUSE, AND IN THE DOOR WALKS BUCK AND A NEW CHARACTER CALLED IRWIN:)

IRWIN

What does Milo see in the Bishop?

BUCK

Well Milo was an altar boy when he was a kid you know, when his father was a bum in El Paso, he's just an old Jesuit, you know, actually .... Besides you know what he does here in this house every night? He's interested in religion, he gets down on his knees with the kids and says the Lord's Prayer and puts them to bed. He really sweetens their cribs.

IRWIN

But I mean that Bishop isnt so much sharp, like we just heard his speech you know, Paul and I were standing in the back and we thought he was a pretty dull sort of ugh bore . . .

BUCK

Sure but it's his wife digs him more . . . Cora, you know

IRWIN

Well, but Milo does too. All this mediocrity that's come later in our lives, when Milo was young and I was young and we kneeled on the dark Texas Plain at night and vowed eternal holy friendship like—you know

BUCK

Well as you say it all goes down the same hole

IRWIN

Hum

BUCK

Think Milo quiter now?

IRWIN

Well I guess he is, ah, but you know didnt I tell you how he came to my pad the other morning, I was playing my Bach Partitas and he started to roll sticks but at the same time he wanted to imitate the unaccompanied violinist but couldnt hardly get the tea out of his little box, when the violin screeched he'd throw up his arms wildly scraping bow on string, tried to lick the paper then the violin began an extended chaconne which left him thrashing on the floor scraping the bow wider and wider—(LAUGHS)—spilled it . . .

BUCK

How *you* feeling?

IRWIN

I'm alright. I woke from a wine drunk 2 AM in the silence of the void birthday night which I'd filled with "woes of the passing wind" the concluding lines of the mysterious Blake Crystal Cabinet a poem I had never understood until that moment like moaning he'd swelt in the crystal cabinet of the mind for years, but—you know, "another London there I saw," I can barely complete a straight line of thought, "when with ardor fierce and hands of flame I strove to seize the inmost form" and so on . . .

(ENTER MILO AND PAUL, A NEW CHARACTER:)

PAUL

Got television Milo?

MILO

Backroom, backroom m'boy, listen here daddies the reason why I wanted to make such fast time back from the lecture, *was,* that I have a little bit of—

BUCK

You left the Bishop a mile down the road there—

MILO

—yes yes, 'bout *five,* miles, actually, *was,* to turn you cats—you know, so as to dig everything, you know, straighten you out, like we're gonna have—like, I'm sick of hanging around here. What's that there you're doing there, what are you talking about there, boys?

IRWIN

I strove to seize the inmost form but burst the crystal cabinet and like a Weeping Babe became a Weeping Babe upon the wild—

MILO

Ah no more poetry for me

(EXEUNT MILO AND PAUL)

IRWIN

Oh God

BUCK

At least the Bishop is coming, huh?

IRWIN

Er, I dont think so, he looks dead

BUCK

Do you like the way he lectures with his eyes closed?

IRWIN

Oh that's just a con routine to impress the women. Did you see all those awful middleaged women sitting there, and old men retired under palm trees and the bullshit he said about astral bodies and auras, why doesnt he just take his clothes off and dance

(ENTER MILO'S WIFE CORA)

CORA

Where's Milo?

BUCK

Backroom

CORA

Milo!

MILO

(OFF) Yes darling!

(EXIT WIFE CORA, ENTER MEZZ, A GUY WHO'S WEARING A BOP CAP, A REAL HEPCAT:)

MEZZ

What's all the action?

BUCK

Did you just get in in your M.G.?

MEZZ

Yeah man, it's outside. Milo said to be here at nine

BUCK

Yeah you're just on time with everybody, s'great

MEZZ

Well man all I need is a little trip to the toilet, I'll be right back. Where's Milo?

BUCK

In the toilet

(EXIT MEZZ)

Do you know Mezz McGillicuddy, that guy? used to be a radio announcer? he's an actor or sumpin? jumps on cars or sumpin?

(THE DOOR OPENS AND IN ENTERS EVERYBODY, THE BISHOP, THE TWO AUNTS, AND BUCK NOW ON HIS HIGH HORSE SAYS:)

Hello! We got here ahead of you!

(RE-ENTER WIFE CORA)

CORA

Wont you sit down, er, Mrs. Bishop why dont you sit on the couch here, and you Mrs. Twidley? Er, ah, you can, sit here, and, can I bring you some coffee?

(AND THE BISHOP, A GOOD LOOKING GUY IN A BLACK ROBE, SAYS:)

BISHOP

Why certainly, may I sit here?

CORA

Oh of course!—so, ah, let's all . . . yes

BUCK

May I sit here on the floor beside you Bishop?

BISHOP

Why certainly! I see you—you are—you have been drinking a little havent you

BUCK

Yes . . . sir . . . but I think that it's alright, I dont, er—we have things to talk about I guess huh?

BISHOP

Yes I understand that you know something about Buddhism

BUCK

Yes I do . . . but I dont know much about Krishna . . . I'm not too particularly interested, either, in Buddhism, actually

(IRWIN FLOPS BETWEEN THE TWO OLD AUNTS WHO ARE SITTING ON THE COUCH AND SAYS:)

IRWIN

Well I'll sit here

(RE-ENTER THE HEPCAT MEZZ)

MEZZ

Well, ah, how d'you do? I'll sit over here, ah, how's everybody?

(AND MILO COMES IN, PAUL COMES IN, AND THEY ALL SIT DOWN AND THE BISHOP IN A GREAT SILENCE SAYS:)

BISHOP

Well!!

BUCK

Yeah!

CORA

Would you like something to drink Bishop? water, coca cola, coffee, tea?

BISHOP

No no thank you, I—I might have a cigarette

BUCK

Bishop (HANDING HIM A CIGARETTE) I'm sure you wont mind if I follow my vice (DRINKING) but I've already poured me a glass of white port hidden in the corner, s'why I wanted to sit here, I've been having a (LAUGHS) hard day . . . . I mean not really, I wanted to sit next to you and ask you a few questions. I wanted to ask you one specific question, do you believe that the universe is infinitely empty or do you think that there's a personal God and we all go back to Heaven to perfection and bliss, that when God shows his Face all our personalities'll vanish?

BISHOP

(PLEASED) Well yes, but there are *stages*

IRWIN

How does one ascend the ladder of doves to Heaven, the silver ladder of Moroccan doves to the great Sherifian Heaven?

BISHOP

Ah Mohammedan, Moroccan, Sherifian, step by step I think

BUCK

Why do we have to take steps? . . . the stages . . . Do you agree with what I'm saying Mrs. ah Bishop, your aunt? . . .

AUNT-I

I ah, I dont know anything about these things

BUCK

You have a very nice nephew

BISHOP

Yes

MEZZ

Here's a cigarette—Oh you *have* a cigarette already, I didn't mean to interrupt, I wanted to give you a cigarette

BUCK

Cora also believes it has to be done in stages . . .

BISHOP

Well that's what I have been preaching, about stages, the Bodhisattva stages, as you well know, being a Buddhist, or having read about it, involves Dhristi . . . . which is spiritual patience . . . We must no expect the Grace of God so soon in a stage of Im-patience you see. It needed, and also is needed Saha, zeal *vitale*

BUCK

Yes

BISHOP

And—precisely—which means we cannot expect salvation, or nirvana, eh, if you wish to call it that, without making some eff-*fort* in the direction of God, some m o v e m e n t (AND HE TWISTS)

IRWIN

Ooh you twisted just like a snake then

BISHOP

Yes?

IRWIN

Yes your movement then was exactly like a supernatural illuminated serpent arching its back to Heaven

BISHOP

Well, ys, probably, of course

IRWIN

I mean that was the *hippest* thing I've seen you do tonight

BISHOP

Well (LOOKING AT PAUL), who's *he*?

BUCK

Oh, that's Paul the saint

BISHOP

Ah! Saint Who?

PAUL

Saint Paul

BUCK

He's a Russian, you know

BISHOP

Ah, a Russian! He has strange eyes and never says anything

IRWIN

He's bashful

BISHOP

Well Paul, what do *you* think?

PAUL

I dont know, I—I think everybody should love everybody, I think that's the only message—It's the only message and nobody ever believes it

BISHOP

Well . . . . and as I was saying there, about Vrykulata, er, the steps towards the heart's desire, you are probably right

BUCK

Isnt that the same as zeal *vitale?*

BISHOP

Yes, but otherwise practicing the ascensions of the stages it requires a great deal of . . .

IRWIN

Olives!

BISHOP

Olives, yes, that's nice. One falls into the danger of becoming bhrasta, no-more-a-yogi, and Pramada is upon us, and, which is cloudness of mind—

BUCK

The constant vision of God in all things and happenings including this moment will prevent us from worrying about cloudy downfalls?

BISHOP

Very wise!

BUCK

What do you think Bishop, am I speaking sense? is it alright if I drink?

BISHOP

You're making sense and you do drink (LAUGHTER)

IRWIN

(TO BISHOP'S FIRST AUNT) Was he always like that as a little boy? Gee he must have been a strange little kid

AUNT-I

Oh yes!

IRWIN

Do you mean—do you mind if I sit between you and your sister?

AUNT-I

Eh, of course not!

IRWIN

(TO THE SECOND AUNT) What *do you* have to say?

AUNT-2

I have nothing to say

BISHOP

Well this is a strange and pleasant evening! .... Let me add, Asagna is not necessary, Asagna is the crosslegged position, as our friend here (BUCK IS SITTING CROSSLEGGED ON THE FLOOR)

BUCK

It's not really necessary, I know it's not really necessary, I just thought I would—I always sit like this at a good party

BISHOP

Very good

BUCK

And since I believe we're all in Heaven now I see no reason

to exercise discipline or worry about it . . . . Would you shut the Gates of Paradise to those who . . *dont* worry about it?

BISHOP

It's not in my power

BUCK

Milo's wife Cora, do you realize the way she is? . . . . she was in such a state of ecstasy the other day that when the children threw rotten eggs in her window she rejoiced in the opportunity God had given her to forgive?

BISHOP

Ah!

(SILENCE, LONG SILENCE)

BUCK

This is what Chekhov called the Angel of Silence, it just flew over us didnt it!

BISHOP

Ah yes . . . And this one here, he never says anything

PAUL

Ah, well . . . . . djeva play baseball? (EVERYBODY LAUGHS)

BISHOP

No, I'm afraid not

PAUL

Did he ever take his clothes off with a girl?

IRWIN

I dont know, ask him . . . Somebody took their clothes off somewhere . . .

PAUL

Bishop I believe in taking clothes off . . . . Do you?

BISHOP

Well, I see nothing wrong with that, of course. I think I'll have another cigarette now

MILO

(LEAPING UP) Any particular brand?

BISHOP

No no, anything

BUCK

Well Bishop, what are we all doing here, and what strange days we live . . . . isnt that so

IRWIN

Yeah, I think we should all be ourselves sometime . . . soon as we can

BISHOP

Yes but as to personal s-e-l-f, it is not something to become attached to as it gives rise to f a w l s e discriminations of the mundane

IRWIN

The mundane's all we got . . . The surface, X, is all we got

BISHOP

Yes but it was given to us by God and by God's omnipotent power—

MILO

Yes!

IRWIN

Well, how are you? (TO THE SECOND AUNT NOW)

AUNT-2

Fine thank you

IRWIN

Er, are we making you unhappy?

AUNT-2

No not in the least

BISHOP

You're all very happy, or if not happy, have v e r v e, you're people with verve

BUCK

Where'd you get that strange accent

BISHOP

Well I'am from Czhekoslovakia. I have to lecture tomorrow afternoon, I think I'd better be going very soon

BUCK

Bishop, let me say, you're positively right in everything you say and you're a very sweet man

BISHOP

My disciple here!

IRWIN

(SINGS) I n t h e p i n e s . . . .

BISHOP

Oh he sings very well . . . You also sing? (TO PAUL)

PAUL

I sing Rock n Roll

BISHOP

Oh can I hear you?

PAUL

Huh?

IRWIN

Go ahead Paul, sing, Rock n Roll

PAUL

Oh no, I dont want to sing . . . . er . . . . I'd rather talk, have you ever read Dostoevsky?

BISHOP

No

PAUL

Do you dream? Djav any dreams?

BISHOP

Yes I dream . . .

PAUL

Can you tell me your latest dream?

BISHOP

Well, er, I guess it doesnt matter very much . . . my dreams are not very important . . . . I dont know. But I did have a dream last night but I'm not sure I can remember it . . .

PAUL

But you gotta remember it! All dreams are holy in the clasel halls of your hort!

BISHOP

I see

PAUL

Grab everybody by the hands and kiss their hands

IRWIN

You should see Paul take his clothes off

BUCK

Ah shut up!

PAUL

Yeah yeah! Do you know about teenagers and how they wanta go to the moon, do you know about masturbation, did you ever walk down the street in the morning and rejoice in the little round asses of girls?

MILO

Erp

CORA

Ur

BISHOP

Well, so, a very strange confusion of ideas!

IRWIN

That was like Bela Lugosi that time . . . Do you think that everything is holy, Bishop

BISHOP

As God's Manifestations yes I think everything is holy

PAUL

Did you read The Idiot?

BUCK

Hey Milo we made it today hey buddy, we made some money in the eighth race didnt we, we made some money finally in the eighth race!

IRWIN

ishop, do you think holy flowers are holy? Do you think world is holy?

BISHOP

Well yes, I think the world is . . . going to be holy

IRWIN

Do you think the alligator is holy?

PAUL

And the hair is holy?

BUCK

Everything holy, Bishop?

IRWIN

Is the Bishop holy?

BUCK

Is Milo holy?

PAUL

Is Buck holy?

IRWIN

Is Paul holy?

BUCK

Is Irwin holy?

IRWIN

Is all holy?

BISHOP

I suppose. I would hope so.

IRWIN

Is Wow holy? I mean is Cora holy? Is holy holy? I mean are the streets holy? Is the ground holy?

BUCK

Is the racetrack holy? Is everything holy? Hooray for holy!

BISHOP

Well yes, I should imagine . . . but perhaps it may be that whatever you want, you'll get . . . . But I really do think I'd better go now

(RISING, AND ENTER THE LITTLE BOY THAT IS MILO'S LITTLEST SON)

MILO

There's my little buddy there, what's the matter boy did we wake you up with all that talk? come on in here son and sit on your father's lap

BISHOP

Ah, he has blonde hair like his mother

IRWIN

Child of light, child of light and gay delight

BISHOP

Good night all of you, I think it's best to go now. I hope to see you all again soon, I hope you come hear my lectures and if you dont want to hear my lectures then at least we've been friends tonight . . .

BUCK

Good night . . . . See you again . . . . (GOODNIGHTS)

(THEY ALL EXEUNT, THE BISHOP, THE TWO OLD AUNTS, PEOPLE LEADING THEM OUT THE DOOR AND BUCK IS SITTING ON THE FLOOR AND SAYS:)

BUCK

The Bishop's alright. Aint nothing wrong with the Bishop.

PAUL

What are we gonna do now, sleep?

BUCK

Well I'm going to sleep out in the yard in my sleeping bag

you sleep on the couch and Irwin sleep on that other couch and Milo's gonna go to bed and Mezz gonna drive back to the city but I'll put on some Symphony Sid on the radio ... Irwin do you think you—for awhile, you know?—did you think you bugged his two aunts sittin like that between em and all that holy avenues of the holy land and the terraces of the temple and all that stuff?—How's things, is everything alright? (HE ASKS MILO AS MILO COMES BACK)

MILO

Aw, the holy straight line of thought ...

BUCK

I think we had a damn good talk. It's alright, Milo. Jesus Mezz McGillicuddy didnt say a word, that's what it's like to be well brought up

MEZZ

Turn that up, man, give me some of that wine. Did I ever tell you show you my cowboy routine? are they gone yet? have they driven out the driveway?

MILO

(LOOKING OUT THE WINDOW) There they go now

MEZZ

[illegible] look—

MILO

Yass, how about some food around here (AS CORA COMES BACK THROUGH THE DOOR), dont we have any f o o d around here?

BUCK

I'm not hungry

IRWIN

I am! Want me to cook it?

MEZZ

—see, my cowboy routine, I come into this dusty old town in Arizona on my piebald pony and get off and go stompin—turn on that radio louder man, that's great, Dizzy Gillespie man!—from the long ride from Flagstaff down to the desert, shake the dust off my hat, walk in the Four Star to slake my thirst, a bittermaker boiling maker maybe two three and there's Blackjack Slim at the end of the bar, "Wal Blackjack it's been a long time" I say and "It's certainly been" says he, "Mezz, how are things in Tombstone, I'm gonna put you right there now," so he's on the move, I see the twitch of his upper lip . . . twisting slightly to my left to give him a thinner profile I swing around and give him my Colt and blast blam blam! twice! for a moment—(BUCK FALLS ON THE FLOOR)—for a moment he leans on the bar as though he was ordering a sh and you hear his gun clatter on the floor, it was half out .

Black Bart lies with his gun still stuck in his holster and beer drooling out of his lips

BUCK

Let me do my cowboy!

IRWIN

Let me do one!

BUCK

Alright you go first!

PAUL

I'll do my Russian cowboy—

IRWIN

—I come to the town, see, from the hills, there are some bushes, I open them real slow and I look and I'm a scissors sharpener and I dance with—and I look down and I peek, I put the bushes aside and I see what they're all doing down there in the town—

BUCK

Wait a minute! wait a minute! I come riding in lookin for my father's killers, I know they're in town, I walk across the dry boards of the sidewalk and my boots clomp and the long spurjingle and push open the swingin doors and there's Bart now, and his brothers and cousins on the side, they've all got their guns out and got me covered and they're all gonna blast me like they done my father . . .

MEZZ

What'd you do then?

BUCK

I turn into a ball of electricity and they all drop dead

MILO

(SUDDENLY) I'll tell you mine . . . . . Preacher ridin into town, I'm standin there at the bar with the preacher as he makes his sermon on the Lord quotin chapter 26 verse 18 in the New Testament "Not a jot and a tittle verily shall ye know that was left" . . . . So there's a drunk in the corner drinkin from his glass sittin crosslegged on the floor drinkin while the preacher makes his speech, I pull out my gun and aim it right at his head and say "Dont you believe in G a w d?" . . . and I let him have it, right through the head

BUCK

(FALLS AGAIN) Ugh!

MILO

Alright you cats, I'm goin to bed . . . . We're all gettin up at six A.M., five-forty-five really, and I'm going to drive you all back to the city

(HE LEAVES, EXITS)

IRWIN

That was strange

PAUL

Where do we sleep tonight?

BUCK

I'll sleep outdoors in my bag, and you guys sleep in these couches . . . . (LAUGHS) . . . I'm *dead*

PAUL

You got another sleeping bag?

BUCK

Naw, I aint got no other sleeping bag . . . you guys go to sleep . . . Why do you think that Milo shot me through the head after this long day that I spent with him . . . . . all the things he wanted me to do and all those Bishops and everything, why did he do that?

IRWIN

Ah he was just demonstrating to you that you're a sinner and you're drinking from the Bishops . . . .

BUCK

Well . . . . I dont know. He had a big day, and he won in the eighth race and he made a little money, I should imagine he'd feel a little happy . . . . but ah *hell*, I'm goin back to the Coast, I'm goin back to Frisco. I'm goin out with this sleeping bag and you know why? when I wake up at 3 A.M. and I dont know where I am and I see all the stars above my sleep I realize what a vast bright room I'm in, the real room . . . . I really sleep out there

IRWIN

Any old room'll do

BUCK

Yeah, but I'm goin

PAUL

(CURLING UP ON THE COUCH) Hope I dream! Dont get cold, Buck, wait a minute now come here Buckie, wait a minute now, good night brother, shake my hand, brother

BUCK

Good night, brother Paul . . . . goodnight, Saint Pau

IRWIN

Goodnight, Buckie

BUCK

Goodnight, Irwin . . . . And I'm goin out there, and you know what I got in my back pocket here, Milo's flute . . . then I'm going across that Holland Tunnel and get on the highway and hide my tail back west . . .

(BUCK GOES OUT)

PAUL

I'll take this blanket. You want this blanket?

IRWIN

No, I've got another one, turn the light off, I'm just gonna nod a little bit here, I'm tired

PAUL

Me too . . . . . . What do you think about what happened tonight Irwin?

IRWIN

I dont know, I guess it doesnt matter . . . It was funny, I guess

PAUL

Bishop huh?

IRWIN

Oh I was bored!

PAUL

When are we going back to New York, tomorrow?

IRWIN

Yeah we're going back with Milo at 5:45

PAUL

Well I guess I'll sleep

IRWIN

We gotta sleep sometime

PAUL

That's right Irwin me boy, I'm going to sleep now

IRWIN

Milo's already asleep, I can hear him snoring

PAUL

Shall I go in and jump in bed with his wife?

IRWIN

(LAUGHS) No never mind . . . . . later

PAUL

Buck's asleep now aint he

IRWIN

No . . . . listen

(THEY HEAR A FLUTE OUT IN THE YARD)

Buck's playing the flute under the stars

PAUL

I wonder why

IRWIN

Must be because . . . he's trying to figure out what all this is all about . . . . whatever it's all about, you know . . . . the world is what form is, and that's all you can say about it, huh?

PAUL

Yeah . . . I guess so. Let's have silent snores, huh? silent snores

IRWIN

Okay

(FLUTE PLAYS, CURTAIN DESCENDS)